# The Trail of Tears

Columbus, OH

SRAonline.com

 **SRA**

Send all inquiries to this address:
SRA/McGraw-Hill
4400 Easton Commons
Columbus, OH  43219

ISBN: 978-0-07-608783-9
MHID: 0-07-608783-2

2 3 4 5 6 7 8 9  NOR  13  12  11  10  09

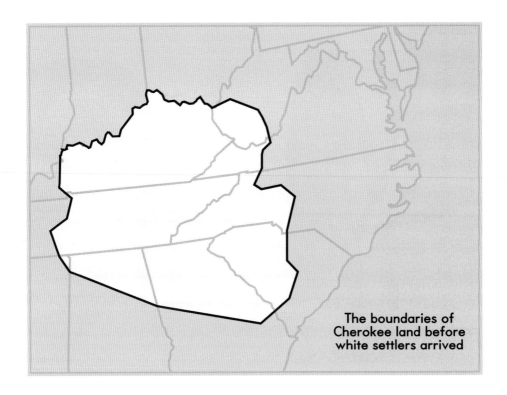

The boundaries of Cherokee land before white settlers arrived

## The Cherokee Nation

When white settlers came to America, the Cherokee had a rich culture and ordered society. They had lived for centuries in the Blue Ridge and Great Smoky Mountains. Their nation stretched from present-day Kentucky to Georgia.

They lived in villages. They grew beans and squash. They raised three kinds of corn. They fished and hunted game for meat and furs. The Cherokee had a government. They held meetings in their capital. The Cherokee lived in balance with nature and each other.

White settlers came around 1673. They brought tools. These made the Cherokee's lives easier. But the settlers also brought diseases. And they wanted land. This made the Cherokee angry.

## Treaties Made, Treaties Broken

The Revolutionary War began. The Cherokee fought on the side of the British. The British said they would help the Cherokee keep their land. But the British lost the war. The Cherokee had to make treaties with the new U.S. government. A treaty signed in 1791 promised peace.

The new treaty explained where the Cherokee could live. It said their land could not be taken. White settlers could not build or hunt on any Cherokee land.

But white settlers still moved into Cherokee territory. The Cherokee fought back so they could keep their land.

Another treaty was signed in 1798. This gave more land to settlers. The Cherokee received goods for their land. They also received a promise of friendship. But the Cherokee's land was becoming smaller and smaller.

## Change

The U.S. government wanted the Cherokee to become more like white settlers. The Cherokee tried to blend the new ways with the old. They built schools and homes like white settlers.

But some refused to change. They left their homes to begin new lives in Indian Territory in the West. They were called the Western Cherokee.

The government continued to break treaties. They wrote new treaties to get more Cherokee land. The government wanted the rest of the Cherokee to move west.

Sequoyah was a well-known Cherokee. In 1821 he developed a way to write down their language. He made eighty-five characters. Each one stood for a sound in the language. Its use spread quickly.

Sequoyah

In 1825 the Cherokee built a capital at New Echota. This area is in Georgia. They used their new writing system to write a constitution. It set up a government. It was headed by a Principal Chief. It also had a judicial branch. The Cherokee began to write new laws.

In 1828 the Cherokee published the first Native American newspaper. They called it the *Cherokee Phoenix*. They wrote the paper in Cherokee and English.

Many white settlers complained about the Cherokee. They wanted the Cherokee to move west.

The U.S. government tried to force more Cherokee to move. But the Cherokee did not want to give up their farms and businesses. They had worked hard for what they had. Besides, their laws said the land was theirs. They would not give it up.

## Gold!

In 1829 gold was found on Cherokee land. The state of Georgia passed "anti-Cherokee laws." The Cherokee could not dig for gold. The laws also let the government take more land.

The state divided up Cherokee land. Land with gold went to white settlers. The Principal Chief of the Cherokees even lost his farm.

The Cherokee asked President Andrew Jackson for help. They reminded him of the treaties they had signed. These treaties gave the Cherokee their land "for as long as the mountains and rivers last."

The first edition of the *Cherokee Phoenix*, 1828

## A New Treaty

But President Andrew Jackson would not help. He signed the Indian Removal Act in 1830. The government could now trade Native American land in the East for land in the West.

This shocked the Cherokee. They desperately fought in the courts to keep their land. But they lost every time.

In 1835 the Treaty of New Echota was signed. The Cherokee gave up the rights to their land. They were paid five million dollars.

Most Cherokee didn't want the new treaty. Major Ridge was one Cherokee leader who signed it. Later he said, "I fear I have signed my own death warrant."

The treaty gave the Cherokee two years to leave their land. The first group left on their own in March 1837. They settled in Indian Territory in Oklahoma.

The remaining Cherokee fought the treaty. Chief John Ross tried to keep his people's land. But President Martin Van Buren said they all had to move.

Chief John Ross

# Removal

In 1838 the U.S. Army moved thousands of Cherokee into forts and camps. "I saw the helpless Cherokee arrested and dragged from their homes," wrote one soldier. There was no shelter or clean water. They had to sleep on the ground. Diseases swept through the camps. About two thousand Cherokee died.

One group of Cherokee in North Carolina would not go. They fought and hid in mountain caves. Because they stayed on their land, they were called the Eastern Cherokee. Their descendants still live in North Carolina.

## Trail of Sorrow

That spring the Cherokee were forced to begin their long march to Indian Territory. "People [felt] bad when they [left the] Old Nation," one Cherokee recalled.

He went on to say that his people wept in sorrow. They said nothing and put their heads down in grief as they left.

The Cherokee were divided into sixteen groups. Each group had around 1,000 people. The first group left in the summer. They battled heat, poor food, and drought. Many of them died.

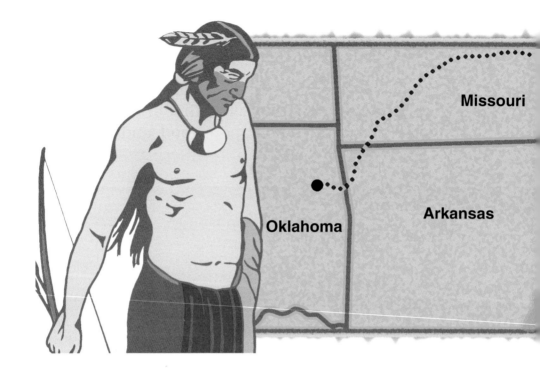

The rest left in the fall. Some took water routes along rivers. Others took land routes. They all traveled during a harsh winter. There were few wagons and horses. Most of them walked.

They walked over 1,000 miles (1,609 km) to their new home. They had to endure hard conditions. One white settler wrote, "Even aged females . . . were traveling with heavy burdens attached to their backs . . . on the sometimes frozen ground . . . with no covering for their feet."

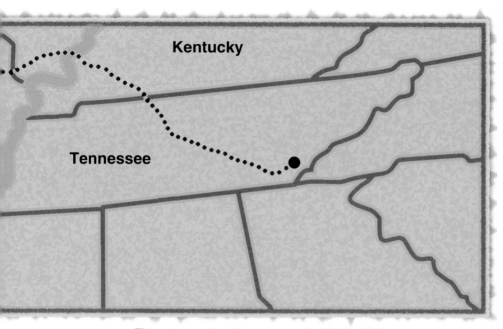

The primary land route on the Trail of Tears

Their trek took many months. They walked through driving rain. They faced knee-deep mud and blizzards. There was little food.

Over 4,000 men, women, and children died on the trail. The Cherokee called this journey *Nunna daul Tsunyi*—the Trail Where They Cried.

In 1987 the Trail of Tears became part of the U.S. National Trails Systems. It crosses nine states. It includes about 2,200 miles (3,541 km) of land and water routes. These routes make up one of the most painful journeys in our nation's history.

# Vocabulary

**centuries** (sen´ chə rēz) (page 3) *n*. Plural form of
**century:** A period of one hundred years.

**territory** (ter´ i tôr´ ē) (page 5) *n*. A large area or
region of land.

**desperately** (des´ pə rət lē) (page 10) *adv*. Hopelessly.

**drought** (drout) (page 13) *n*. A period of time when
there is very little rain or no rain at all.

**endure** (in dûr´) (page 14) *v*. To put up with.

**trek** (trek) (page 15) *n*. A long, slow journey.

# Comprehension Focus:
# Drawing Conclusions

1. Reread page 10. What conclusion can you draw
   about why President Jackson signed the Indian
   Removal Act?
2. On that same page, what conclusion can you draw
   about what the Cherokee hoped would happen when
   they went to court?